R.A!R.A!
A Meeting Wizard's Approach

by Shirley Fine Lee

BookSurge Publishing, LLC
An Amazon.com Company
Charleston, SC

Published by
BookSurge Publishing, LLC
An Amazon.com Company
7290 B Investment Drive
Charleston, South Carolina 29418

To order additional copies of this book, go to www.Amazon.com

ISBN 1-4196-5367-9

R.A!R.A! A Meeting Wizard's Approach

Cover design by Miriam Langer and Jonathan Lee.
Wizard illustrations and web graphics created by Jonathan Lee exclusively for Shirley Fine Lee.

About The Author

Shirley Fine Lee has worked as a training and development specialist since 1986, and an independent consultant since 2000. She has extensive experience, helping organizations with their team building, training development, meeting facilitation, presentation delivery, and other communication needs. This work involves developing productivity tools, presenting workshops, and writing. For instance, she has authored numerous training manuals and guides, on a wide variety of topics. Shirley holds a Bachelor of Arts degree in Management Information Systems from Dallas Baptist University. She has received a corporation's Quality Excellence and Customer Satisfaction awards, and is a member of the American Society for Training and Development (ASTD), for which she writes articles.

Acknowledgements

Thanks to my husband, Dan, for encouraging me. Thanks to my son, Jonathan, for enhancing my ideas for Wizard graphics and making them a reality. And thank you to Miriam Langer for graphic design expertise. Also, thanks to all those numerous people who have had faith in my ability to lead meetings and training classes, as well as those who encouraged me to lead teams and projects.

Table of Contents

Preface

Why did I choose a Wizard as my icon for this book? Definitions of wizard from *Merriam Webster's Collegiate Dictionary* include "a wise man; one skilled in magic; a very clever or skillful person". To me the wizard indicates one with a great skill. Whether that skill is to create magic, manage time, organize workspace, enhance meetings, or complete projects - the skill is the key to success.

When you get control of your time, it will magically seem like you have more time to accomplish important tasks. When you organize your workspace, you accomplish things more quickly by knowing where to find necessary items. When you have control in meetings, not only do you accomplish more in less time but you also bring a skill that can be learned by others through observation. When you properly manage a project, you may become considered wise and skilled in this area and then be asked to manage other projects, which increase in importance.

Each of the planning skills may build upon the others. Having an organized workspace can help with time management. Knowing time management basics can help with project management. Recognizing the importance of personal time and the time of others can help with meeting management. See the diagram of Interconnectivity of Planning Skills for a picture of how building skills upon each other could work.

Interconnectivity of Planning Skills

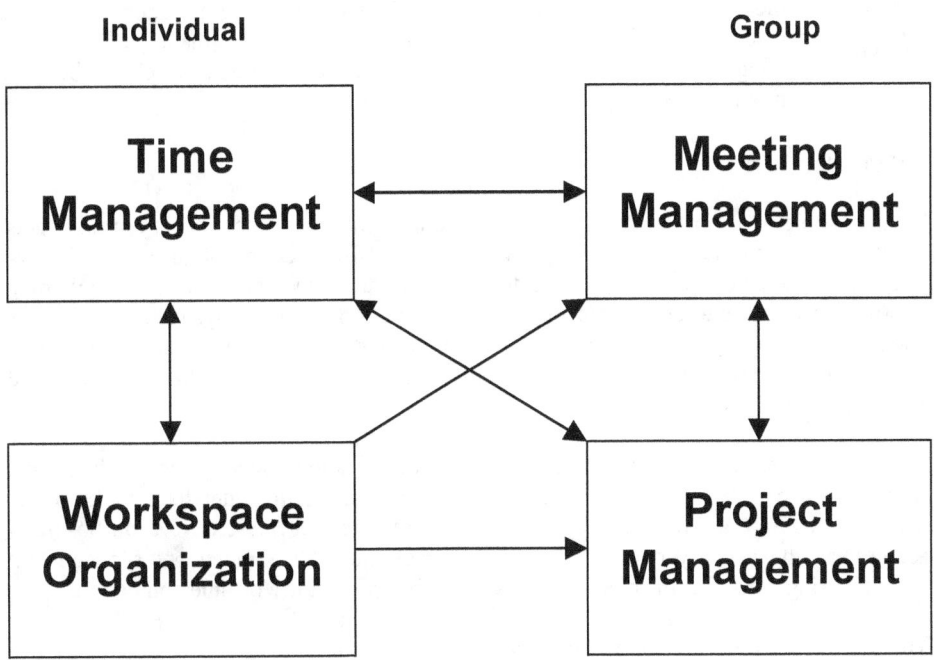

In the diagram above the arrows will represent how one planning skill can help to build or improve another. A two-way arrow indicates having a skill can help with the improvement of another skill and vice versa. For example, having individual time management skills makes one more aware of their time and the time of others. Therefore, time management makes the individual want to improve their time use in their workspace as well as working in groups on meetings or projects. Conversely, having a better-organized workspace and knowing how to manage meetings or projects can result in a better use of time. Another example is knowledge of meeting management can lead to better project facilitation and knowing how to assign people to project tasks can result in better meeting follow-up. A one-way arrow indicates that the skill the arrow goes from helps in improvement of the skill at the arrows point. For example, knowing how to organize a workspace can result in better project or meeting management as the needed items are where it is most convenient for the individual or group using them.

When is it a good idea to practice meeting management?

When you need to accomplish a goal within a meeting timeframe or need multiple people to participate in the meeting's process you should manage meetings using the R.A!R.A! approach. Good meeting management results in ideas generated, problems resolved, decisions made, tasks assigned, and higher member feeling of accomplishment, which can be a morale booster.

Introduction

Many people do not enjoy attending meetings because they feel nothing gets accomplished and therefore their time was wasted. If this feeling of "a waste of time" continues, it often causes a greater waste of time by the reluctant members complaining to others about the ineffectiveness and mismanagement of the meetings they attend. This book is a quick study in basic meeting management and the necessary related skills. This book also includes sample formats that may be useful in practicing the principles and skills outlined.

People who feel meetings are a waste of time, need to know meetings are an important way to get ideas shared and important tasks accomplished. In order for people to feel their meetings are a valuable use of their time, the meeting must have a purpose and accomplish the primary purpose within the timeframe of the meeting. Management before, during, and after the meeting is essential for efficient use of time and people.

The objectives of this book are to spend a few hours learning:
- The basic principles of meeting management
- The necessary meeting roles as well as what types and methods exist for meetings
- How to prepare for meetings by:
  - Getting the right people there by proper use of notifications
  - Planning ahead using a checklist
- How to use the R.A!R.A! approach (Roles, Agenda, Records, Actions) to:
  - Start and end meetings on time
  - Accomplish more in each meeting by keeping on track
  - Insure meeting ideas and decisions are captured
  - Accomplish needed tasks and follow-up outside the meeting
- What problems may detract from meetings and how to deal with them
- How to improve future meetings
Then summarize the key points and basic principles.

Successful meetings accomplish the desired results (tasks assigned, problems resolved, ideas generated, decisions made) while working together as a group using an agreed upon process. Not everyone will always be happy about the outcome of a meeting, but if the meeting process is results-oriented and decisions are typically by consensus, then most members attending the meeting will feel they contributed and the time was worthwhile. Resources and time wasted by people gripping about having to attend the meeting or carry out the results of the meeting will be less likely to occur if members felt a valuable part of the meeting.

Basic Principles

The following principles are the basic structure of Meeting Management:

- **All members must agree on meeting purpose, agenda, and desired accomplishments.** If the group needs to generate ideas, resolve a problem, discuss issues, or share information, all need to agree that is the primary purpose for coming together at the time designated.
- **All members must agree on how to accomplish the purpose(s) of the meeting.** The group needs to agree upon which process, method, or procedure to use in order to generate ideas, solutions, or share information important to the meeting tasks.
- **All members must be willing to take action in and outside of the meeting in order to accomplish the purpose(s) of the meeting.** The group needs to determine necessary processes to use in the meeting and assign tasks for accomplishment outside the meeting.

Keep in mind the following supportive principles when trying to manage meetings.

- **During meetings, everyone must have a role to play and the group must understand the purpose of each role.** Roles must include a facilitator, recorder, and members. Other roles, such as observer may apply as needed by the group. One person may take on more than one role if agreed to by the group. For example, the facilitator may also act as the recorder.
- **If the meeting has no goal to accomplish or no agenda, then the meeting has no real purpose.** Therefore, cancel additional planning for the meeting.
- **Meeting records are important to achieve problem resolution and track results.** In other words, someone should be keeping track of what is going on in the meeting and the results of the meeting. Distribution and storage of the meeting results need to occur in the form of minutes as soon as possible after the meeting.

Purpose

Before planning a meeting, a clear purpose for meeting must be determined. A manager or designated person, prior to a meeting, may determine the primary meeting purpose or the members of the meeting may decide what the final purpose will be. Either way, the first thing the meeting group should do in their meeting is agree to the meeting's purpose.

The purpose is a simple written statement of why the group is getting together. If the group cannot agree to a common purpose, then the meeting or series of meetings are doomed to failure. Once the purpose is apparent, then the details of the meeting in an agenda format and an estimation of how many meetings are necessary to accomplish the purpose can be determined.

Value

A meeting's value to the organization relates directly to how effective it is at accomplishing the meeting purpose. If the meeting accomplishes 40% - 60% of its purpose, which is about average, then the cost of having the meeting may be balanceable by its benefits. If the meeting accomplishes less than 40% of its purpose, the cost of the meeting is generally a loss. If the meeting accomplishes more then 60% of its purpose, then the meeting was beneficial and the cost of the meeting is an investment in the organization. To increase the value of meetings, an approach for increased participation and effectiveness is imperative.

Effective Meeting = Investment	**100%**
Average	**50%**
Ineffective Meeting = Loss	**0%**

Cost

Is the meeting's purpose and potential value relevant enough to merit the cost of holding a meeting? This is a hard question to answer, however using a formula to calculate the cost of a meeting and then weighing that against the expected benefits may help. To determine the actual cost of a meeting, find the following data: an approximate average hourly rate for each person attending the meeting (R) and a count of the number of people expected to attend the meeting (N). Then multiply those numbers to compute total attendee cost (AC). Then take the number of hours (H) the meeting will be to multiply by the total attendee costs to compute approximate meeting cost (MC). An example of the formula follows:

$$AC = (R \times N)$$
$$MC = H \times AC$$

R.A!R.A! Approach

The R.A!R.A! (pronounced Rah! Rah! like a cheer) approach to better meeting management refers to using pre-assigned meeting Roles, having an Agenda, keeping Records of what goes on in a meeting, and assigning Actions as items or tasks to be accomplished outside the meeting. The R.A!R.A! approach contains the key elements and measures of the entire meeting management process. Utilizing two or more of these will increase the productivity of meetings. Utilizing all the elements and measures of R.A!R.A! will make meeting results more effective. Adding additional meeting planning and follow-up activities will increase productivity and effectiveness even more.

3

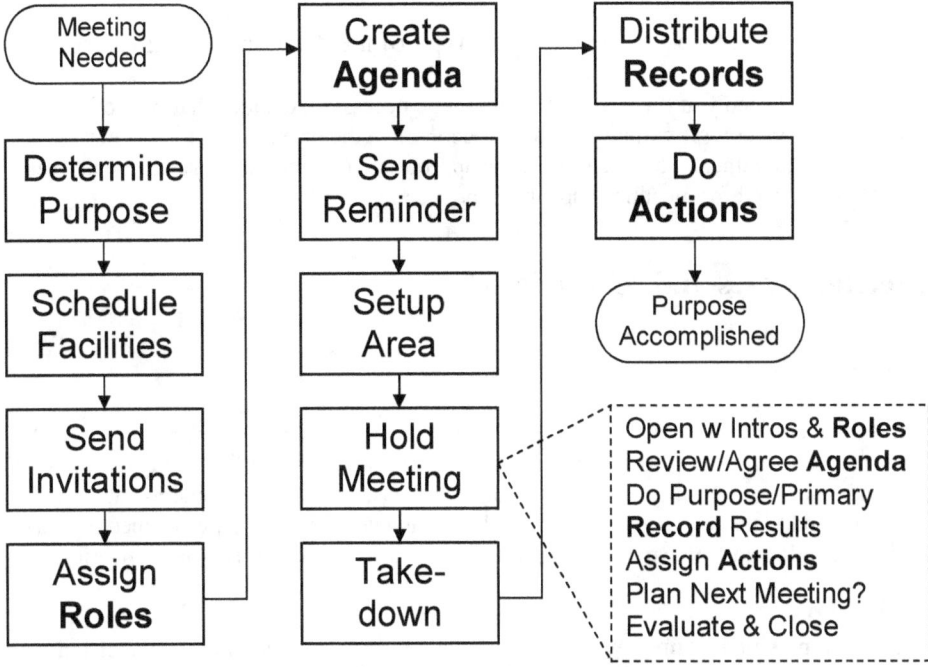

The flowchart of R.A!R.A! approach within the meeting management process indicates typical order in which planning, holding, and follow-up happens for meetings. The dashed line box is the order in which the held meeting should follow for greatest success. Detailing of each of the elements and measures of the R.A!R.A! approach will be later in this book.

When do you decide what type of meeting or method to use?

When you think a meeting might be necessary, decide what type of meeting it will be in order to accomplish the primary purpose of getting together. Then determine the appropriate method that best fits the delivery need for most participants in the meeting.

Meeting Types and Methods

Types

There are many different types of meetings. These types differ in their purpose as well as what processes may help to accomplish the purpose. Meeting utilization is typically for briefing each other on information, sharing ideas, resolving problems, or making decisions and plans that affect the group. Following are the basic types of meetings with their description and an explanation of when to have or not have this type of meeting.

Decision-Making

A decision-making meeting reviews different alternatives and then makes a decision by a specified deadline on which alternative(s) to select. This type of meeting should be held if the group is required to make and then support or carryout the decision. If the group is not the primary decision maker, then the decision maker must participate in the meeting, otherwise the meeting should be for list generation or problem solving instead. Decisions may result in a problem to pursue, data to gather, or a solution to try. Once reaching a decision, the group needs to determine what actions are required to carry out the decision and then assign the tasks. If there is no follow-through on the decisions made, then it will be the same as if no decisions existed. Therefore, the meeting members will feel their time was wasted or their group is ineffective.

> **Common decision-making methods (in order of group desirability) include:**
> - **Consensus**
> - **Unanimous Vote**
> - **Majority Vote**
> - **Weighted Voting**
> - **Committee / Sub-team**
> - **Management**
> - **Minority**
> - **Apathy / Avoidance**

Do not hold a decision-making meeting, if group cannot agree on a primary and back-up decision method to use or if the decision was already made and the only purpose is really to get agreement to or compliance with the decision. Doing this only causes distrust in the person calling the meeting or suspicion that group or meetings are not truly effective. In other words, do not plan a decision-making meeting as a method of pushing through a preferred idea.

List Generation

A meeting may exist simply for generating a list. This could be a list of product ideas, potential problems, possible solutions, service requirements, or any other type of list. After creating the list a discussion may follow in the same meeting, prioritizing or voting on the list items may occur, the list may go to someone to work with, or planning of another type of meeting may follow for utilizing the list. When listing items, do not place names next to the suggested items because once an item is on the meeting list, it becomes the groups instead of belonging to the individual member. List generation can be in a single meeting typically lasting no more than an hour or two, such as a designated committee or focus group, or it can be a part of a different type of meeting.

> **The most popular method for generating a list in a meeting is "brainstorming", in which each member contributes ideas to the recorded list until no one has any ideas left to add. During "brainstorming", members may not criticize or comment on each other's ideas during the listing process. However, members may suggest new ideas building on those ideas submitted by others.**

List generation should not be continuous meetings to add to the list. Typically, this is a one-time meeting to generate the desired list relating to a particular topic. Once the list generation is complete, that particular meeting need is over. Do not plan a list generation meeting if members each agree to come up with a specific number of items for the list and then post the list for the group's review. If the desire is to have customers, co-workers, or suppliers generate a list without their having to spend time in a meeting, then a questionnaire may be an alternative. The questionnaire is distributed, and results compiled without a meeting. If a questionnaire is used, those getting the questionnaire need to be given a date when their response is expected.

Problem Solving

Problem solving meetings are for definition, research, analysis, and eventually solving problems that may exist. These problems could reference production, quality, services, or other things. In order for problem solving to work, those closest to the problem must participate, in other words representatives of each area affected by the problem should agree that a problem exists and be involved in finding the solution. Problem solving requires a defined process and method to root out the true problem and then find the best solution(s). This process must include important decision makers, preferably in the whole process or in at least the specific meetings where a decision must occur. Problem solving typically takes several meetings as issues may come from outside the group, data must be gathered and analyzed, and potential solutions need to be tested. Then a meeting for results review and decision-making is in order to insure the solution works and is accepted. Over the course of the problem solving process, various types of meetings or portions of the meeting will be involved, such as list generation, decision making, and planning.

Problem solving meetings should not occur if many do not believe there is a problem or are unwilling to work on finding the root of the problem and committing to changing things to solve the problem. Problem solving meetings should not turn into multiple briefings or status sessions, as this can hinder motivation to get the problem resolved. Nor should problem-solving meetings be a method to push a certain perspective, force a decision, or resolve personal conflicts. In order to insure problem solving results are not off-track and will be more generally accepted, it is a good idea to share meeting minutes with those that may be affected by the problem and potential solutions but do not participate in the meeting.

> **Problem solving typically involves these steps:**
> 1. **Define Problem**
> 2. **Analyze Causes**
> 3. **Gather Data**
> 4. **Generate Solutions**
> 5. **Evaluate Tests**
> 6. **Realize Implementation**

Project Planning

Project planning meeting members are usually those people assigned to work on a particular project or task. The meeting may start out as list generation of what tasks need to be done, then as the list is evaluated the tasks are typically broken into categories or phases. Completion of certain tasks or phases may be designated milestones. Finally, after getting estimated timeframes, the project team members get task assignments. Additional meetings may be for project plan updates, solving problems, reviewing budget, celebrating accomplished milestones, and evaluating risks.

Project planning meetings are not necessary if the project or task only requires one person to complete. Project meetings shall not occur if the only reason for meeting is to status where the project is. Project status can be accomplished by having the project plan updated by the project manager on a server where all team members have access to it or by the sending of a memo or electronic mail (email) on a regular basis to members and interested parties. However, a short project status

> **Project planning typically involves these steps:**
> 1. **Open and analysis of project feasibility.**
> 2. **Plan approved project schedule, resources, and budget.**
> 3. **Implement project plan via defined execute and monitor processes.**
> 4. **End project by completing management actions.**

or progress review as a briefing in management meetings may be appropriate occasionally. Sometimes, these briefings will require the project team meet to update their plan and discuss what problems, issues, or risks need to be in the review for management awareness.

Strategic Planning

Strategic planning meetings are typically annual meetings and their design is to determine vision, goals, business ventures, and other items related to the future of a company or group. The strategic planning meeting may be one long meeting or several meetings spread out over a specified period. After defining the strategy, then a communication plan or deployment plan is developed, then future meetings are typically status of plan accomplishment, problem solving, or other needed revisions to the strategy and therefore no longer called strategic planning.

> **Common results of strategic planning sessions include:**
> - **Vision**
> - **Values / Beliefs**
> - **Mission / Purpose**
> - **Goals / Objectives**
> - **Process Maps**
> - **Policies / Procedures**
> - **New Business**
> - **Change Plan**

Do not utilize strategic planning meetings for designated projects, although a project update, project designation, or high-level project design may come out of a strategic planning meeting. Strategic planning may include problem solving or process changes at a high level, but the details are typically an assignment to another person or group to work outside the strategic meeting.

Briefing

Sometimes people call meetings because a small or large group needs to come together for sharing information. However, in informational sessions the group members usually do not actively participate, therefore a better reference instead of meetings is briefings, since their primary purpose is to brief on, supply status, or provide information in a quick and concise summary method without participation from members. In briefings, members are not participating instead they are acting more in the role of observer or audience. Sometimes a briefing will have a question and answer period at the end or after specific presentations. However, this question and answer period is controlled by the person briefing others and not controlled by the members. This is a way to allow the briefing person to elaborate and provide more detail on the information important to the audience rather than for the purpose of participation in the meeting.

A presentation may be necessary to get buy-in or commitment for pursuing the problem to solution or for approval to proceed. If it necessary to have presentations during a meeting or if planning a briefing instead of a participative meeting, plan the presentation so everyone gets the most from it. The presentation may be in written form, such as a paper, or it may be someone delivering the information with supporting graphics. Find out if a presentation or paper is necessary and when the expected delivery date is. Then prepare a presentation using a format, which may also be useful as an outline for a paper.

Short presentations may exist in participative meetings, but should not be the primary reason for those meetings. Participative meetings are those where all the members may provide input to the result or product of the meeting. In addition, it is not cost effective or time efficient to have a briefing for informational purposes if the communication of information may be appropriate via a letter, internal memo, email, or other documentation. If the purpose of the meeting is to present new information on which many questions may be expected, then a briefing may be appropriate to save time by not having to answer the same type of questions multiple times. However, if the purpose of the meeting is only to allow the audience to see the person giving the briefing, then a video or internet/intranet offering, which may be viewable at audience convenience, may be an alternative to consider in lieu of a live setting. If desired, these alternatives could include a supplemental questionnaire form that allows the audience to send questions in which replies or clarification will come later via web posting, email, or internal memo.

Example Presentation Plan

Page 1

Date of Presentation: April 10	Time of Presentation: 9:15-9:45
Location: Building A, Room 21	(When to be there?) 5 minutes early

Primary Topic: Review problem analysis and determine potential solutions.
Audience: Problem Solving Team   Decision-Makers: Mike and Tim
(Mike, Sam, Sherry, Stan, Sue, Teri.
Tim, Todd, Tom)

Purpose/Objective: Review results of problem analysis and begin next step in problem solving process

Outline:
Reasons (Why are we here?)
• To review and discuss problem analysis, then pursue and implement solutions
History (What have we done?)
• Reviewed problem solving methods and decided to use D.A.G.G.E.R. process
• Had meeting to determine what type of problems exists and how to track their occurrence
Future (What do we plan to do?)
• Select problem area to pursue
• Brainstorm and select potential solutions
• Test solutions.
Recommendations/Alternatives (What have we learned?)
• Summarize chart data and team recommendations
• Ask problem solving team to determine what to pursue and resources to request
Research/Data (What do we have to share?)
• Consolidation of tracking and cost data from Sam, Sue, Stan
Resources (What do we need?)
• Recommendations from Sam's and Sue's teams

Proposed Delivery:		
Topic item:	Talker Assigned:	Time Allotted:
Review results of problem analysis	Frank Franklin	30 minutes

Supporting Documents:		
What item:	Who Assigned:	When Due:
• Track number of occurrences for Research Problem #1	Sam	4/1
• Track number of occurrences for Research Problem #2	Sue	4/1
• Determine approximate cost of each type of problem occurrence	Stan	4/1
• Sum data in worksheet and create graphs	Wanda	4/7
• Visuals – Create slides from graphs and text	Frank	4/9
• Handout Materials – Copies of 2 slides per page for each attendee	Frank Franklin	April 10

Question and Answer period

Potential Questions:	Proposed Answers:
• Why is the number of occurrences of problem #1 so high on Tuesdays?	• Sam will explain Tuesdays are new hire training days for all locations.
• Why does 3rd item on Problem #2 cost so much?	• Stan will explain single vendor for part
• Why do we need 3 new people to solve Problem #1 when part of the problem is training new people?	• Sam will have to research if true solution.

Presentation Plan Format

Page 1

Date of Presentation: Location:	Time of Presentation: (When to be there?)
Primary Topic:	
Audience:	Decision-Makers:
Purpose/Objective:	

Outline:
• Reasons (Why are we here?)
• History (What have we done?)
• Future (What do we plan to do?)
• Recommendations/Alternatives (What have we learned?)
• Research/Data (What do we have to share?)
• Resources (What do we need?)

Page 2

Proposed Delivery:		
Topic item:	Talker Assigned:	Time Allotted:
Supporting Documents:		
What item:	Who Assigned:	When Due:
• Visuals		
• Handout Materials		
Question and Answer period		
Potential Questions:	Proposed Answers:	

* NOTE: It is permissible to copy this form for meeting/ briefing use as practice. *
R.A!R.A! A Meeting Wizard's Approach

Methods

There are various types of meetings and different methods exist for the various types. The meeting method selected will depend primarily on how much interaction is required for the meeting, what equipment and facilities may be available, and how to review in-meeting result records.

Face-To-Face

A face-to-face meeting is the standard where everyone meets together in the same room to hold a meeting. The advantages of this method are everyone sees each other and sees presentations or posted meeting results at the same time. A disadvantage may be lost time and extra expense of travel if group members must come from locations far away.

Net Meeting

A net meeting or an on-line meeting is one using computers as the meeting method. It can include email, instant messaging, chat rooms, web pages, or video display. Documents used for visuals or discussion may be read-only or interactive and could consist of text, graphics, or slides. Special software, computer microphones, video cameras, phone lines, network connections, internet connection, and/or large projection screens may be requirements for this meeting method. Depending on what options are available for this type of meeting, the advantages and disadvantages may be the same as teleconferencing or videoconferencing.

Teleconference

A teleconference is a meeting where all or most members call via phone into the conference call or meeting room in order to attend the meeting. Special conference telephone lines and setups may be required to hold this type of meeting. Speakerphones and headsets may be utilized to make being on the phone for a continued time easier. When using a teleconference, a disadvantage may be that others are not visible, therefore body language may not be interpretable or the speaker may not be recognizable if they do not introduce themselves before talking. Other potential problems are people talking over each other, interruptions in remote offices and associated noise coming into the meeting, and it may be hard to keep pace for recording results. To prevent problems with data communication, use the computer or fax to provide data before or during the meeting, preferably before if possible. An advantage of this method is reduced travel costs.

Videoconference

A videoconference is a meeting where members call into the meeting from meeting rooms with special video and audio capabilities. Most of the advantages and disadvantages of teleconferences also apply to the video conference, except possibly for not being able to see the person speaking. An additional disadvantage of videoconferencing is delayed transmission. Sometimes someone at one location may begin to speak on a topic while someone at another location is talking about something else but neither knows due to delayed reception. Therefore, people at both locations may be confused once they hear what they expected to be a response to what they said. If using videoconferencing, be aware of possible time delays and exercise patience.

When should meeting preparation and notification occur and what does that mean?

When you want a successful meeting, you should prepare for it. Preparation includes assigning a facilitator, making sure the room and equipment are appropriate, that invitations and/or reminders are prepared, as well as planning the agenda and for someone to record what happens. For members, preparation means scheduling the time for the meeting, reviewing any relevant materials and completing assigned actions before the meeting.

Preparation and Notifications

Preparation

In preparing for a meeting, be sure to schedule the meeting at the best time and place for the group members. Most people are fresher in the mornings; therefore, this may be a better time for idea generation or problem solving. Afternoons are more hectic and people tend not to want to take too much time during this period, therefore it may be best for briefings or quick meetings where there is a concern that the invited members may talk too long on a subject. However, do not plan a meeting directly after lunch if there will be multiple presentations, as people tend to be less attentive at this time. When planning where to have the meeting, keep in mind accessibility by members and necessary equipment along with any setup requirements. Creating or using a meeting checklist for typical setups can make meeting planning easier.

A list of possible preparation questions to ask when planning a meeting appear on the following table. This list includes categories of items such as meeting roles, methods, types, and planning for potential problems. It also includes communications or forms that may be useful in preparation and planning including: checklists, agenda, notifications, records, and actions. After the question table, follows preparation related to facilities, materials, and equipment.

Example Meeting Preparation Questions

Category	Questions
Actions	What are possible outcomes and actions of the meeting? What is process for action assignment? Will there be agreement and clarification on the actions necessary as well as whom will be responsible for each action and their due date? When is a reasonable timeframe for completion of the actions inside and outside the meeting? If people not at the meeting have an action, how are they to find out about their action, the reason for the action, and when it is due?
Agenda	What is the purpose of the meeting? What are to be the meeting accomplishments? In what order should items flow? How long will the meeting be? How much time is allowable for each item? What should occur during opening and closing of the meeting?
Checklist	Is a standard checklist available for meetings of this type? Should a specialized checklist be prepared for the meeting?
Equipment	Is any special equipment necessary for meeting? Is the equipment at the facility? If not, do we bring or rent equipment?
Facilities	What type of facility bests fits the meeting needs? What is the process to schedule the facility? How much time is required for the facility, including setup and takedown time? Where are closest restroom and refreshment facilities? Where is smoking allowable in or around the facility? What is organization policy regarding smoking in meetings? Can food and drinks be in the meeting area? Should refreshment provision be part of the meeting costs? Will anyone need to travel for this meeting? Are special travel arrangements or accommodations required?
Materials	What are the materials necessary for the success of the meeting? Will the materials be provided prior to or at the meeting? Does a checklist for provision of materials exist?
Methods	What meeting method will best suit the purpose? What will the overall costs of holding the meeting in dollars and time be verses the benefit of holding a meeting?

Notifications	What types of people need to be there or who needs to participate in meeting? Who must be present in order for the meeting to start? Will cancellation of the meeting result if these people will not attend? How will meeting notifications be done and who will do them? Is any special information or reports necessary for the meeting? Should this information be available prior to the meeting? How are members to know of information to review prior to meeting? If special travel arrangements are necessary, will information be included in notifications?
Problems	What might go wrong in or during this meeting related to issues, people, environment, etc.? What is the plan for dealing with what goes wrong?
Records	How will meeting accomplishments be recorded? Is the necessary in-meeting record keeping items on checklist and provided in facility?
Roles	Who are the assignments of facilitator and recorder roles? Who will play what other meeting roles in the meeting? Is there any special information these people need to do those roles?
Types	Is a meeting necessary to meet the purpose or is another approach better? What type of meeting or approach best fits the purpose and members?

Facilities

When preparing for a meeting, the person planning the meeting should try to schedule a facility or room that is close to where most of the group will be coming from and is large enough for the entire group but not too large that it will restrict communication. Also, determine whether a writing surface for the members or observers is necessary. The room should have the same amount of chairs as members, including the facilitator and recorder in case there is a break where they can sit down for a few minutes. If the meeting is to include multiple presentations, then at least two extra chairs need to be available for those presenting, who come prior to their scheduled time, to sit and wait their turn. The room lighting should fall in areas where members will be looking. If necessary, windows may require covering to prevent group distraction.

To insure room is ready for the meeting, the facilitator and recorder should arrive at least an hour early and plan to stay up to an hour after the meeting for takedown to return room to original order and copy down records. This will also allow extra time for finding replacements for any required removed equipment from the facility or if the required equipment is broken. Therefore, the meeting room scheduling needs to be for up to an hour before meeting to do setup and for an hour after meeting to takedown records and put room back in order.

Equipment

In addition to seating in facilities, make sure the room has any display equipment needed for the meeting, such as computers, projectors, boards, or flip charts, as well as appropriate pointing devices and markers in multiple colors. Make sure the necessary equipment, both hi-tech electronic devices and low-tech manual items, are available in the room or facility where the meeting is to be. If these are not available, then make sure the equipment is available prior to meeting and that it will work in the room. If the room does not have the appropriate electrical setup, move to another facility or consider revising the format of the meeting. The checklist format suggested at the end of this section has some equipment listings along with space to add items. However, a checklist that fits the meeting group's specific needs may need to be developed. If not sure what the room has, go over a checklist with the contact person for the facility or room to insure what is available and what other arrangement may be necessary.

Materials

Any materials that need review before the meeting or are for use in the meeting by the members need to be part of their meeting invitations and reminders. Whoever is responsible for distribution of pre-meeting review materials needs to be aware of their responsibility and carry it out. Often this is the meeting planner, but another person may have the responsibility as an action from a prior meeting. The meeting planner, facilitator or recorder should be responsible for follow-up on review materials and all other items, including equipment, needed to insure the meeting's success. Other item responsibility includes board markers and erasers, spare pens or pencils, extra paper or transparencies, items to post meeting results, and cleaning supplies such as paper towels or wipe cloths.

Anyone planning to speak or present should plan to bring any handouts they want to distribute or make sure the planner, facilitator, or recorder got a master in order to make copies. Delivery of the copy master needs to be to the person responsible for distribution at least two days in advance of the meeting to allow time for getting copies.

Setup

The facilitator and recorder need to arrive at least an hour before the meeting to make sure room arrangement and equipment is appropriate to the type of meeting. If not, this will allow time for moving things around and finding missing equipment. In addition, the facilitator and recorder can place any materials at each seat prior to the meeting or determine what will be handouts during or after the meeting and how the handouts are to be distributed. If need be, request some members arrive early to help with the setup; however, all should arrive on time. Everyone involved in the meeting should prepare for the meeting, whether scheduling, setting up, or reviewing data prior to start. Allowing time for setup insures the start of the meeting is not late due to improper setup or late arriving members.

Takedown

The facilitator and recorder need to plan at least an hour after the meeting to make sure room is back in original order, retrieve records, and see that trash is appropriately tossed. This reference for return of room to original order process is called takedown. Takedown is a consideration for the next user of the room as well as making sure records of meeting are retrievable.   If some members were able to provide help with setup, those same members may be willing to help put room back in the original order. Facilitator and recorder will also be responsible for packing and removing any extra materials, as well as getting recorded items from boards written down or taking paper sheets for development of minutes.

Checklist

A checklist is an efficient tool to accomplish verification of all items related to meeting preparation.   Experienced facilitators will often create and use checklists that are specifically for their most common meeting types and methods.   A checklist will typically include requirements for facilities, equipment, and materials. Following is an example of what a completed checklist might look like.

Example Checklist

Name of Facility: Building A, Room 21
Contact: Wanda Writer   Phone: 555-555-5555 X 5
Meeting/Briefing Date: April 1
Start/End Times: 9:00AM-11:00AM   Setup/Takedown: 8:00AM / Noon
Number of Chairs: 11   Number of Tables: 0
Description or Drawing of Table & Chair Arrangement:
Place flip charts (FC) on either side of screen with the transparency projector (TP) between and
to the back of charts. Place one chair on both sides of the projector and other chairs in semi-
circle facing the flip charts.

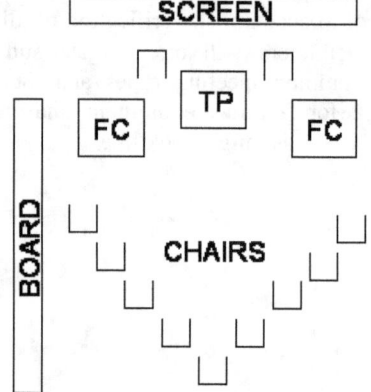

Instructions on how to get to facility/room (or where to ship materials):
From lobby of Building A facing receptionist, go up the stairs on the right. Once on the 2nd
floor, turn left and down the west hall. Room should be 3rd door on right side of hall.
Equipment needed in Facility/Room:

Hi-Tech	Indicate Number	Low-Tech	Indicate Number
Audio/CD Player	N/A	Marker Board	1
Computer(s)	N/A	Flip Charts	2
Projection Device	N/A	Chalk or Markers	Multi-Markers (Dry Erase & Flip Chart)
Projection Screen	1	Cleaning Supplies	Paper Towels
Transparency / Overhead Projector	1	Tape, Clips, or Push Pins	2 Rolls Masking Tape

Materials to be brought or shipped to Facility/Room:

Transparencies	4 (Problem Study Graphs)	Flip Pages from last Meeting.	2 (Solution List)

Checklist Format

Name of Facility:	
Contact:	Phone:
Meeting/Briefing Date:	
Start/End Times:	Setup/Takedown:
Number of Chairs:	Number of Tables:

Description or Drawing of Table & Chair Arrangement:

Instructions on how to get to facility/room (or where to ship materials):

Equipment needed in Facility/Room:

Hi-Tech	Indicate Number	Low-Tech	Indicate Number
Audio/CD Player		Marker Board	
Video/DVD Player		Chalk Board	
Computer(s)		Flip Charts	
Projection Device		Chalk or Markers	
Projection Screen		Cleaning Supplies	
Transparency / Overhead Projector		Tape, Clips, or Push Pins	
Laser Pointer		Hand-Held Pointer	

Materials to be brought or shipped to Facility/Room:

Books		Handouts	
Transparencies			

* NOTE: It is permissible to copy this form for meeting/ briefing use as practice. *
R.A!R.A! A Meeting Wizard's Approach

Notifications

Another important aspect of meeting preparation is to be sure everyone understands the purpose of the meeting by calling potential members or by sending notifications to the appropriate people. Pre-meeting notifications include invitations and reminders. If possible, include the purpose and agenda in pre-meeting notifications, as this will help people focus on what exactly are the accomplishment goals and objectives for the meeting. By providing this information, potential meeting members will know if they should attend the meeting, send someone else, or decline representation at the meeting. Meetings work best if the right people are present, and if preparation and organization occur prior to the meeting. Preparation includes sending notifications and preparing an agenda. Assignment of roles, such as facilitator and recorder, and actions due may be in the notifications.

Invitations

When sending a notification inviting people to participate in a meeting, be sure to let them know if they need to review anything prior to or bring anything to the meeting, such as copies of a report sent to them earlier or copies of the last meeting minutes. The initial meeting invitation should go to everyone who is to be a participating member of the group. Non-participators, such as observers or people giving presentations may also be on the invitation. To save people's precious time and prevent confusion, typically invite only people who have something to contribute to the meeting's purpose or are regular members of a group. On the invitation, be sure to correctly spell names, include time and location of meeting, meeting purpose, and agenda if available. Where possible, send the invitation at least two weeks prior to the initial meeting to allow people to arrange their personal schedules.

If group members plan to send electronic mail (emails) regarding their meetings to one another, then the person responsible for most transmissions may want to look into methods that will reduce time sending these emails. One method is if the group members are using the same network application that includes a time management/scheduling tool and it is part of an integrated email or contact system, these tools often have a built in method of scheduling a meeting at a time open to most members. Once the meeting is scheduled, these applications typically will send automatic invitations to the members selected to attend the scheduled meeting. Use of these tools can save time in creating the invitations especially if the application allows the user to input their own text in the invitation. If the group does not have a networked application, then the person responsible for invitations may want to investigate how to save time creating emails by setting up group email identification (ID) in their email application, electronic contact database, or electronic address book. A group email ID is a single identifier typed in "to" address that will automatically find all associated email addresses of members to send a copy of the email.

Example Invitation

Subject: Meeting Invitation for 04/01 at 9:00 AM

Your experience and/or expertise are necessary for a successful solution. Therefore, you are invited to participate in a meeting with the following purpose in mind:

Purpose: Review problem analysis and determine potential solutions.

The meeting will be held at the following time and location:
Date: April 1
Times: 9:00am-11:00am
Location: Building A, Room 21

If you feel this contact is in error or prefer to send another representative to the meeting, please pass the meeting details onto that person and then contact the person sending this message as soon as possible. Thank you for your anticipated participation in the success of this meeting.

Regards,
Wanda Writer 555-555-5555 Extension 5

Reminders

Since sending of meeting invitations is as far in advance of the meeting as possible, reminders are necessary to insure no one forgets to attend. Reminders may be via phone calls a few days before the meeting, or they may be in written or electronic form. Conveying a reminder should be at least two days prior to each meeting. The reminder should include the agenda, who will be doing which roles, actions that are due prior to the meeting, and any items the members need to bring. As noted in invitations above, some applications that can send electronic versions of invitations may allow automatic reminders as well. In some applications, the reminders may be set to transmit automatically on a specific date and time. Often these reminders only remind of the meeting time and place and do not allow for additional text. Therefore, if users plan to send the agenda in the reminder, the automatic reminder option should not be selected and the person responsible for reminders should manually plan and do the reminder task.

Example Reminder

Subject: Meeting Reminder for 04/01 at 9:00 AM

Thank you for agreeing to share your experience and/or expertise in our meeting. Below are the meeting details so you may prepare in advance of the meeting.

Purpose: Review problem analysis and determine potential solutions.

Materials To Review/Bring: Review problem study graphs emailed as attachments earlier in the week and potential solution list on last meeting minutes.
If you did not receive the materials, please let the person sending this message know so the materials may be sent to you.

The meeting will be held at the following time and location:
Date: April 1
Times: 9:00AM-11:00AM
Location: Building A, Room 21
Directions: From lobby of Building A facing receptionist, go up the stairs on the right. Once on the 2nd floor, turn left and down the west hall. Room should be 3rd door on right side of hall.

Roles: Facilitator - Frank Franklin, Recorder – Wanda Writer

Proposed Agenda:
Members   Introductions, Review Agenda, Review Actions   9:00-9:15
Frank   Review results of problem analysis (graphs)   9:15-9:30
Members   Discuss list of potential solutions   9:30-10:15
Members   Narrow solution list to 3 items to test   10:15-10:45
Members   Assign Actions, Plan Next Meeting, Evaluate/Review 10:45-11:00

If you have any questions, please feel free to contact the person sending this message or the meeting facilitator.

Thanks,
Wanda Writer 555-555-5555 Extension 5

Cancellations

If canceling the meeting, instead of a reminder, a cancellation notice is the requirement. Send this notice as soon as meeting cancellation occurs. Early notification will allow potential members to re-evaluate their individual scheduling plans. The cancellation should include a brief statement as to reason for the cancellation, such as the problem no longer exists, delay of the project, key members are unavailable at this time, facilities or equipment not available, etc. If another meeting is to be scheduled, include this fact in the notice and the planned future meeting date. Again, this is to let the members know in order for them to update their schedules accordingly. If sending a cancellation notice stating the proposed new date and time, then another invitation may not be necessary. However, it will still be necessary to send a reminder prior to the new meeting date.

As noted in invitations and reminders, some applications that can send electronic versions of invitations may allow for automatic notice of meeting cancellations. Some electronic cancellations may allow additional text inclusion to explain the cancellation or give other types of information. Therefore, if the electronic cancellations do not allow text input and the user wishes to explain the cancellation, the automatic cancellation option is not viable and the person responsible for the cancellation notice should manually do the cancellation notice.

Example Cancellation

Subject: Meeting Cancellation for 04/01 at 9:00 AM

We are canceling our meeting due to key members' inability to meet together with the customers on this date. Below you will find details on the cancelled meeting and the proposed rescheduled date.

Cancelled Date:	April 1
Times:	9:00am-11:00am
Location:	Building A, Room 21
Proposed Date:	April 15
Times:	9:00am-11:00am
Location:	Building A, Room 21

Thank you again for your willingness to participate.

Regards,
Wanda Writer 555-555-5555 Extension 5

Thank You Notes

If the meeting was a one-time event or multiple meetings where the project has completed, be sure to thank those who participating in making it a success. If a member of the group did outstanding work or provided important details, thank them in the meeting and if appropriate send a thank you note afterwards as well. If appropriate, copy the individual's supervisor on the thank you note. If someone outside the group gives a briefing or presentation, be sure to send a thank you to that person. Recognizing people for their contribution and thanking them for giving help or information makes people more willing to help again in the future. Sending thank you notes can be a member assignment as a meeting action or may be primarily the responsibility of the facilitator or recorder.

Example Thank You Note

Subject: Presentation given on 04/01 at 9:00 AM

We wish to thank you for taking the time to come to our meeting and provide our group with information on the use and costs of the XYZ machine. We recognize the major effort on your part to put this information into a presentation format that would contain all necessary data and be easy for us to understand. This information was instrumental in our discussion and decision making process.

Thank you again for your willingness to help us.

Regards,
Frank Franklin 555-555-5555 Extension 2
Manufacturing Problem Solving Team

 When is it a good idea to utilize a standard approach with roles?

Whenever you want a meeting to be effective in accomplishing its purpose, an approach such as R.A!R.A! should be utilized to insure better meeting management. Not only does using a good approach improve your meetings but wise use of roles aids in accomplishing goals.

Roles

An important part of the R.A!R.A! approach is to understand the roles utilized to make meetings more successful, as these will be referred to often in this book. Assigning these roles is the first preparation element to consider in the R.A!.R.A! approach. Members of the group or people outside the group may take on these roles. However, once a meeting has started with each person taking a specific role, no person should change their role within the meeting unless they get permission from the group to do so for a period of time or on a specific topic.

The meeting management principle tied to roles is during meetings, everyone must have a role to play and the group must understand the purpose of each role. The roles may have different names and some groups have many more roles than those defined here. In order to understand the roles throughout this book, the roles will be referred to with the generic "_r" version of the names. It is ok to utilize more roles, such as timekeeper or gatekeeper, if a group feels it is necessary. However, this book will only specify the major roles needed to insure a successful meeting. These major roles are Facilitator, Member, Observer, Recorder, and Talker, which follow in detail.

Facilitator

The facilitator is someone who guides the meeting process and insures that it flows according to the agenda or that the group agrees upon a change to the flow. The facilitator may offer suggestions for how to proceed by suggesting methods or processes to use, but does not participate in the discussion and decision making processes. This person may act as gatekeeper letting members know when they have strayed from the agenda, subject, or selected process. The facilitator also acts as timekeeper to insure adherence to the agenda timeframes or that changing the timeframes is agreeable to all meeting members. This person makes sure everyone participates and may act as protector to insure there are no personal attacks between members and that conflicts are resolved quickly or set aside for the meeting. The facilitator should be responsible for making sure facilities, equipment, and materials are appropriate to type of meeting planned.

When should a facilitator not be a member of the group? If everyone in the group wants to participate actively in the meeting, without looking as if a particular group member is "in charge" or "pushing their views" then the facilitator should be independent of the group. On the other hand, when a topic may get emotional or controversial and someone impartial is necessary to insure things do not get out of hand, then an independent facilitator is a good option. Another occasion for an independent facilitator is when a person with facilitation skills is necessary to insure process flow, adherence to the meeting agenda, provide options for methods and techniques to use in problem solving or decision making, and still allow all members to participate equally.

Member

The meeting members are the people who are active participants in the meeting. They understand the purpose of the meeting and related problem or issue. Members are there to provide input and ideas, do research, take actions, and help with decision-making. They also let the facilitator, observer, or recorder know what is expected of them prior to the meeting and if that person steps outside their assigned role during the meeting. Members are also responsible for the meeting flow toward achieving purpose and for listening respectfully to one another.

Observer

An observer is someone who attends the meeting as a quiet member of an audience. It could be someone who sits and observes a small meeting in order to provide input on problems later. This may be an expert, who is there to answer questions from the group throughout the meeting. This could be a group of people attending a meeting for informational purposes. Observers are not to participate at all in the meeting unless called on or not until the end when an open questions and answer period may be permissible.

Recorder

The recorder is a person or persons who may act as a scribe by recording items on large sheets of paper or writing boards, including action items. This person may be responsible for taking and publishing minutes. When recording items, recorders use the member's words and ideas without changing the meaning or text, but do not list the name of member stating it. However, the recorder may use abbreviations or acronyms agreed to by the meeting members. The recorder may help the facilitator with setup and takedown of facilities, equipment, and materials as appropriate to the meeting. The recorder can be someone who is independent from the group or a member. The role of recorder may rotate amongst group members, as long as all members use the same format for recording meeting results and for minutes.

Talker

A talker or presenter could be a member who is providing a presentation or sharing data during a particular portion of the meeting. The talker could be someone who attends the meeting only for a given amount of time to provide information to the group. This may be an expert, who is there to present information or answer questions from the group during a specified time in the meeting.

Example Role Rotation

Member Name	Meeting Dates				
	April 1	April 8	April 15	April 22	April 29
Frank	F	R	M	M	M
Sam	M	F	R	M	M
Sue	M	M	F	R	M
Stan	M	M	M	F	R
Wanda	R	M	M	M	F
Role Rotation: F = Facilitator, M = Member, O= Observer, R = Recorder, T = Talker					

When should an agenda be part of a standard approach?

Whenever you want a meeting to accomplish its purpose, an approach that emphasizes using and following an agenda, such as R.A!R.A!, should be utilized to insure effective meeting management. Not only does using an agenda help to organize a meeting, it can be useful in focusing participants during the meeting.

Agenda

The creation and use of an agenda is the second preparation element in the R.A!R.A! approach. Prepare the agenda as far in advance of the meeting as possible in order to include it in meeting notifications. Preparing an agenda for the meeting will help keep it on track. An agenda ties to the meeting principle of if the meeting has no goal to accomplish or no agenda, then the meeting has no real purpose. Therefore, an agenda is important to insure meetings not only start and end on time but also accomplish something in between those times. An agenda may cover several topics or one topic with various parts. Whether it is several topics or a single topic with various parts, each will have an assigned timeframe on the agenda. The meeting facilitator should provide an agenda to the meeting members prior to the meeting. If an agenda is not available before the meeting, the members should ask for it before the meeting begins.

Each meeting should open with a review of the agenda and agreement to any changes. If an agenda is not prepared prior to the meeting, the first few minutes of the meeting must be dedicated to coming up with and agreeing to an agenda. Having agendas posted in the meeting equates to the following meeting principles all members must agree on the meeting purpose, agenda, and desired accomplishments and all members must agree on how to accomplish the purpose(s) of the meeting.

The best time to prepare an agenda for the next meeting is during the closing few minutes of a meeting. After the assigning of actions, then the meeting members need to help create a tentative agenda for their next meeting. This agenda creation process should be quick since the members will have mentioned things throughout the meeting that may need discussion on or work sessions for later. If there are too many items for desired meeting time, have the group decide which one(s) may be moved two or more meetings in the future. If there are presentations on the agenda, see if there may be a place where it may be appropriate to reduce the time. If reducing time on an agenda, it is better not to reduce discussion and decision time unless group is sure that the smaller amount of time will still accomplish a good result.

If there are not enough items to take the desired meeting time, ask the group to come up with more items to add to the agenda, select items from future items or issue list or parking lot, adjust topic timeframes realistically, or agree to have a shorter meeting. The reason the members should help create the agenda is the meeting is theirs and therefore the responsibility for what it accomplishes is theirs. The facilitator does not own the agenda nor creates it alone. However, the facilitator may suggest processes to use in order to accomplish the desired agenda items. After choosing the agenda items, then the group should decide what order the items should take on the agenda. Do they want presentations first since the data may be necessary to make a decision or is there some agenda item that is critical and important that they need to insure accomplishment of it early just in case they need more time for that item?

3 T's

Things or items that may need discussion or work sessions in future meeting agendas include get and review data, have someone present, make a decision, or other items listed on the records of the meeting. At the end of a meeting, pull these future items out and determine when to tackle them. Decide if these things should be on the next meeting agenda or in a later meeting. After assigning the recorded items to a meeting, then ask the group to assign the three (3) T's as appropriate to the next meeting agenda. The three T's are the Talker, the Topic, and the Time limits for each item. The Talker is the person who is responsible for the agenda item or who is planning to present or speak on the agenda topic. The Talker may be blank if the topic belongs to the group, such as brainstorming ideas, or the Talker designation can be Members" or "All". The Topic is the subject of the agenda item. Topic includes how to handle the item. Handling may include what process to use, such as brainstorming solutions to a specified problem. The Topic should be written using action words, such as discuss, decide, present, etc. Finally, the Time limit can be the estimated timeframe in minutes for a tentative agenda or approximate start and stop times for final proposed or published agenda.

When asking a non-member to present as a Talker insure a member takes the action to notify the Talker of their Time and Topic as soon as possible after the meeting in which a presentation request arose. This way the Talker can let the member or facilitator know if they cannot make the desired meeting time or if they will need more or less time for their presentation. Be sure the Talker knows to allow time for questions and answers.

Opening

Always start the meeting at the designated time on the notification and follow the agenda. Otherwise, people will think it is ok to be late and the meeting will not accomplish all the agenda items. Starting on time and allowing five to fifteen minutes, depending on meeting length, for opening the meeting and setting the mood for the work will let members know it is a serious meeting. If assignment of roles did not occur prior to the meeting, then their assignment is the first meeting item before proceeding. If the members do not know each other or if there are observers/talkers present, then introductions are next on the agenda. If this is the first time the group will meet, it is a good idea to add a few minutes to the agenda for establishing a code of conduct or ground rules for meeting behavior. After roles and introductions, then the group reviews and revises agenda as needed, including resetting time limits for each item.

If a member comes after the opening and wants to add an agenda item, this is not allowable, as it does not encourage on-time arrival for the next meeting. If members often have something urgent to share, then have a "new business" time on the agenda that occurs at the end of the meeting in which they can give a short report and ask for discussion or advice. Finally, the rest of the meeting should follow the agreed to agenda. Be sure to post the agreed upon agenda where all members can see it. Check items off the agenda as they are completed. This way if anyone comes late or has to leave the meeting for a few minutes, the individual can see where the meeting is without having to stop the flow to ask what is going on.

Closing

Depending upon how long the meeting is, allow five to fifteen minutes at the end of the meeting agenda for closing the meeting and planning what happens next. First, make sure to assign and record action items, including who will send appropriate "Thank You" notes to Talkers. Then determine when and where the next meeting will be. Then the group should develop a tentative agenda for the next meeting using the three T's. If the group wants to track how their meetings are improving or how they work together as a team, then an evaluation at the end of the meeting is appropriate. Be sure the meeting has a positive close by restating the meeting purpose and quickly reviewing the meeting accomplishments towards that purpose.

Primary (In Between)

Between the opening and closing of the meeting, the primary purpose for the meeting is accomplished. In the primary portion of the meeting agenda, members need to stay focused on the topic or problem at hand. To the best of their ability, they should follow the agenda they agreed to during the meeting opening. Having a facilitator role assigned will aid in keeping to the agenda.

If this is the first meeting of the group, it is a good idea to take a few minutes to establish a code of conduct or ground rules for meeting behavior. Then members can use the ground rules in addition to the agenda to help stay focused and respectful of one another during meetings. Once the members have agreed to the agenda and ground rules, the responsibility for the meeting and all that does or does not get accomplished becomes theirs. If confusion on an issue arises, the members need to insure they are all working on the same thing and not on different items. Using the recorder role with large paper or a writing board to record meeting ideas and decisions will help members to stay focused.

However, if it seems like the meeting is getting off track and the facilitator has not noted this to the group, then a member should point it out so the group can review where they are and how to continue.

Example Tentative Agenda

Meeting Purpose: Review problem analysis and determine potential solutions.		
Date and Time: April 1 9:00AM-11:00AM		
Location: : Building A, Room 21		
Talker	Topic	Times
	Opening:	
Members	Introductions, Review Agenda, Review Actions	15 mins.
	Primary:	
Frank Franklin	Review results of problem analysis	30 mins.
Members	Discuss list of potential solutions	30 mins.
Members	Narrow solution list to 3 items to test	30 mins.
	Closing:	
Members	Assign Actions, Plan Next Meeting, Evaluate/Review	15 mins.

Example Proposed/Published Agenda

Meeting Purpose: Review problem analysis and determine potential solutions.		
Date and Time: April 1 9:00AM-11:00AM		
Location: Building A, Room 21		
Talker	Topic	Times
	Opening:	
Members	Introductions, Review Agenda, Review Actions	9:00-9:15
	Primary:	
Frank Franklin	Review results of problem analysis	9:15-9:45
Members	Discuss list of potential solutions using Like/Dislike	9:45-10:15
Members	Narrow solution list using Weighted Voting (3 votes per member), then Reach Consensus on to 3 items to test	10:15-10:45
	Closing:	
Members	Assign Actions, Plan Next Meeting, Evaluate/Review	10:45-11:00

Agenda Format

Meeting Purpose:		
Date and Time:		
Location:		
List Topics, then note Talkers, and then assign Times		
Opening:	Introductions, Review Agenda, Review Actions	
Talker	Topic	Times
Closing:	Assign Actions, Plan Next Meeting, Evaluate/Review	

* NOTE: It is permissible to copy this form for meeting/ briefing use as practice. *
R.A!R.A! A Meeting Wizard's Approach

When is it important to record meeting results in an approach?

When you want to track your meeting accomplishments, a record of the meeting is important to capture items such as ideas generated, decisions made, processes or diagrams designed, and action items assigned. The R.A!R.A! approach stresses that participatory meetings should have a record of their results.

Records

Having an agenda is key to getting the meeting off to the right start and keeping it on track. Keeping records during the meeting is also an important key to making sure the meeting focus stays on track to agenda topics. That is why records are the first subsequent measure of the R.A!R.A! approach. These records are a valuable resource for tracking the results of meetings during and after. In the meeting, records may be on some sort of writing board or paper version, such as a flip chart. Keeping records of meeting results tie directly to the principle meeting records are important to achieve problem resolution and track results. After the meetings, those same records go through conversion into a distributable form, commonly referred to as minutes. Distribution and storage of minutes may be on paper or electronically.

Boards and Paper

It is important to have a recorder use some sort of writing board, such as chalk, marker, or electronic version to record meeting progress. Alternatively, paper flip charts or large sheets of paper taped to walls may be useful to record meeting progress. This captures meeting items so they help keep the minds of members attentive during the meeting. It keeps the members focused on the current topic and selected process. Capturing items also reduces repetition and adds a sense of accomplishment as the group can see all that they have done during the meeting.

When recording ideas, try to use different colors or bullets to specify when addition of different ideas go onto record. This makes it easier for the group to see the division of items instead of everything being a blur of text. Also, do not put the names of members who state items next to items because once the item is recorded it belongs to the group. Write names only in relation to action items. If a member has something that may be hard to put into understandable words, encourage them to go up and draw a picture to insure the group gets their meaning. The recorder should write down exactly what the member says and not edit their words. If the recorder incorrectly captures something, the member is responsible for politely correcting the mistake. Since meetings often move faster than the recorder can write, use of common abbreviations and allowance for misspelled words need to be agreeable to the group. When the team makes a decision or selects items, circle them or mark them with group assigned priority numbers.

Which is better to use, boards or flipcharts? Marker boards or chalkboards are nice to put agendas on, as they are visible by all and easily edited if the group decides to change the agenda before the meeting gets going or during an important discussion, that needs extended time. These boards may also be useful to capture meeting progress. However, before erasing the board, insure the person responsible for minutes has copied the board onto paper. Chalk tends to be less easily seen and messier than using a dry-erase maker board. Therefore, the marker board is the preferred of the two board types. Be sure to bring the proper type of markers to the meeting so board is not ruined.

The advantage to using paper flip charts or large sheets of paper taped to the wall over boards is they are portable and semi-permanent. When the captured items are on large paper, the papers are then easily movable around the room for future reference as the meeting progresses. Then after the meeting, take the paper outside the room for transfer to a distributable minute format. For subsequent meetings on continuing projects, the paper copies may also be usable again in later meetings on the same topic. Be sure to use markers on the paper that write thick and dark enough for seeing from the other side of the room, but that will not bleed onto walls. Also, write a page number in the upper left corner of each sheet so the sheets may reflect the order the meeting progressed through. Numbering the pages will also allow members to select only specific sheets to return with the facilitator or recorder to subsequent meetings.

Minutes

Minutes serve as a valuable record of what happened in the meeting and who is responsible for actions items from the meeting. Groups occasionally refer back to historical meeting minutes to verify decisions made, review ideas, and/or select next problem to work on from a previously generated list. After the meeting is over, the meeting records should become minutes by transcription into a savable and distributable format. Minutes are then available to members via paper or electronic versions. Minutes may also be available to talkers and others who may be interested in the meeting or project outcome. Whatever method in which published minutes are distributable, they should be available as soon as possible after the meeting. Publication within a day of the meeting is best or two days at the most.

If the meeting progress record is on a permanent writing board in the meeting room, then the recorder or assisting member should transfer data to paper before erasing the board to continue and before leaving the meeting room. If the meeting record is on large sheets of paper, then the recorder may take the sheets and re-order them for production of minutes. If any of the sheets or a requested summary sheet is to be available at the next meeting, assign the recorder or facilitator responsibility for insuring the maintenance of the sheets or the making of a summary sheet. The responsible person will then bring the sheets to the group's next meeting. When developing the minutes, the recorder should correct misspellings and spell out abbreviations since people reading the minutes may not remember or know their meaning.

Minutes can include the following types of data: meeting agenda, meeting attendees, primary purpose of meeting, processes used, ideas generated, decisions made or deferred, actions assigned, presentation summaries, and the next meeting date with tentative agenda. The recorder should design a minute format that is agreeable to the group. The format should include major headings that help members quickly find specifics in the minutes. Headings and sub-headings can be data type or category specific and/or subject specific. Headings also allow non-members to find items that they are interested in from the meetings without having to read everything. For example, managers may want meeting specifics like what statistics were available, what process utilization was, what test processes will be, or what decision-making occurred in the meeting.

Example Minutes

Page 1

Meeting Date/Time: March 1/9:00-11:00 AM   Location: Building A, Room 21

Meeting Date/Time: March 1/9:00-11:00 AM   Location: Building A, Room 21

Purpose: Agree on meeting purpose and generate potential manufacturing problems.

Roles: Facilitator - Frank Franklin   Recorder - Wanda Writer

Attendees: Mike, Sam, Sherry, Stan, Sue, Teri. Tim, Todd, Tom

Agenda: Talker	Topic	Times
All	Introductions and review roles	9:00- 9:15
Members	Agree on Meeting Purpose and Problem Definition	9:15- 9:30
Frank	Explain Brainstorming	9:30- 9:35
Members	Brainstorm list of potential problems	9:35-10:00
Frank	Explain Weighted Voting and Consensus Decision-making	10:00-10:05
Members	Reduce list of potential problems to top 2 or 3 using Weighted Voting	10:05-10:15
Members	Discuss how to measure top problems and reach Consensus	10:15-10:45
Members	Assign Actions, Plan Next Meeting, Evaluate/Review	10:45-11:00

Process/Results:

Brainstormed list of potential problems and number of weighted votes:

• Too many people doing same job	2	
• Not enough people on Manufacturing line	1	
• Procedures not well defined	4	(RP#2)
• Procedures not always followed	5	(RP#2)
• Conveyor belt gets jammed	4	(RP#1)
• Conveyor belt moves to fast	3	(RP#1)
• Quality Control not in Manufacturing area	1	
• Containers sometimes break	1	
• Containers are too small	0	
• Manufacturers not properly trained	1	
• People aren't motivated to do it right	0	
• Too much rework on items	2	
• No way to tell what steps are being done	5	(RP#2)
• No way to tell when a step was completed	4	(RP#2)
• Conveyor gets hot after 3 hours of running	3	(RP#1)

Decisions:
- Will combine three Conveyor items into research problem #1 with checklist to track how many times each item will occur.
- Will combine procedure/step problems into research problem #2 by having a copy of procedure steps move along with item on manufacturing line. Each time a step is done, manufacturer's initials and completion date must be placed next to step on procedure copy. If a step is deviated from, line person needs to write reason for deviation. This way we can track what is done and what needs to be changed or clarified on procedure.
- We will graph tracking data to verify type of each problem that occurs most often and each one's related cost.
- After data review, we will determine which problem to discuss for possible solutions.

Definitions:
- Consensus means all agree they can live with and support decision.
- Weighted voting will be each member getting to a place a single vote on a designated number of items on a list (4 per member for this meeting). Then the items with the most votes will be finalized list for review/use.

Evaluations:
- Evaluated meeting using an evaluation form tallied at end of meeting. Reviewed results and found we felt Roles and Process were above average for this meeting. (Overall Rating = 2.1)

Actions: Who	What	When
Sam	Track number of occurrences for Research Problem (RP) #1 for 1 month	04/01
Sue	Track number of occurrences for Research Problem (RP) #2 for 1 month.	04/01
Stan	Determine approximate cost of each type of problem occurrence	04/01
Wanda	Graph results of problem tracking	04/07
Frank	Make transparencies of graphs and bring to second April meeting	04/10

Next Meeting Date/Time: April 1   /   Tentative Location: Building A, Room 21
9:00-11:00 AM

Purpose: Review problem analysis and determine potential solutions.

Roles: Facilitator - Frank Franklin   Recorder - Wanda Writer

Agenda: Talker	Topic	Time
Members	Introductions, Review Agenda, Review Actions	15 mins.
Frank Franklin	Review results of problem analysis	30 mins.
Members	Discuss list of potential solutions	30 mins.
Members	Narrow solution list to 3 items to test	30 mins.
Members	Assign Actions, Plan Next Meeting, Evaluate/Review	15 mins.

Minutes Format

Page 1

Meeting Date/Time:		Location:	
Purpose:			
Roles: Facilitator		Recorder	
Attendees:			
Agenda: Talker	Topic		Times
Processes/Results:			

Page 2

Decisions:		

Actions: Who	What	When

Next Meeting Date/Time:	Tentative Location:

Purpose:

Roles: Facilitator	Recorder

Agenda: Talker	Topic	Time

 When should actions be given during a standard meeting approach?

When you want activity to occur outside the meeting in order to completely accomplish the purpose of meeting, then actions must be assigned. An effective meeting approach, such as R.A!R.A! will always encourage the recording, assigning, and tracking of action items.

Actions

It is important to record actions in the meeting records, while the meeting is going on and afterwards in the minutes. Action assignment and accountability is the second subsequent measure of the R.A!R.A! approach. So be sure to communicate due actions when meeting reminder notifications are sent. Actions or action items are tasks that members will do outside the meeting in order to accomplish the meeting purpose or group goals. Actions tie to the meeting principle all members must be willing to take action in and outside of the meeting in order to accomplish the purpose(s) of the meeting.

Be sure to record actions on a board or paper during the meetings, including actions for thank you notes and notification of presentations by non-members. After the meeting, the actions transfer to the minutes and then actions that are due by the next meeting appear on that meeting's reminder. Having actions on the reminder gives members a chance to get the action item done before they have to report a status. Additional actions that may appear on the meeting reminder include any data the members should review before the next meeting, including reviewing results of a prior meeting.

3 W's

In order to insure that action items are clear, assignment using the three (3) W's guideline is necessary. The three W's stand for Who, What, and When. Who should do the task? What is the task to do? When is the due date on the task? In addition to the three main W's, some groups add a fourth W standing for Where is the task as a status section for member accountability and acknowledgement purposes. The Where section would indicate where the item is in the work cycle: started, in work, completed, or deleted. After actions have been marked completed or deleted, they will not appear on future minutes or reminders for the group. If the group chooses to assume actions that are not deleted or completed are to be in work, then they may just use those two statuses and replace the When date with the status on the meeting minutes rather than having a fourth column. Only due actions should appear on reminders. Only actions still open should appear on minutes for meetings after the minutes that originally recorded the completion or deletion of an action item.

Example Actions

Meeting Date or Project Name: March 1		
Who	What	When
Sam	Track number of occurrences for Research Problem #1 for 1 month	04/01
Sue	Track number of occurrences for Research Problem #2 for 1 month.	04/01
Stan	Determine approximate cost of each type of problem occurrence	04/01
Wanda	Graph results of problem tracking	04/07
Frank	Make transparencies of graphs and bring to 2nd April meeting	04/10

Actions List Format

List what actions are to be done, then add the names of who will do the action and when they will have it done by.

Meeting Date Or Project Name:		
Who	What	When

When can you tell that the meeting process is threatened and items may not be accomplished?

When you see disruptive or uncooperative behaviors or a lack of energy in members, it is a sign that the meeting may be in jeopardy. It is important to understand how these problems may occur and how to handle them.

Beastly Problems

Even if all the elements and measures of the R.A!R.A! approach and other hints in this book are used, problems may still occur in occasional meetings. When a problem occurs in a meeting, it usually throws the meeting off and creates a high stress level for some members. Problems can also cause the meeting results, if any, to be of lower quality than a meeting where focus and motivation to accomplish the same things is in everyone present. It is important to remember that everyone in the group is responsible for insuring successful meetings and anyone should feel free to point out if they notice a problem may be occurring. The facilitator typically does this, but if the facilitator does not know the group or issue, they may take longer than a member to notice a problem is beginning.

It is not always easy to spot a problem before it escalates. When problems in a meeting occur, people leaving the meeting may jokingly say things like "what a circus" or "it was like a zoo in there". This is because it felt like the animals took over the control of the meeting rather than human beings. How can spotting of animals in meetings before it is too late to capture and resolve the problem occur? Watch for the occurrence of any of the following to tell if the meeting has a problem. Then decide which options for working around or through problems best applies.

Darting Deer

A member that darts into meetings after they start or leaves early, or gets up to answer pages or make phone calls often unknowingly disrupts the meeting. Their inability to commit to the meeting timeframes is disruptive to the group. It sends the message "I've got better things to do." This member needs to realize they are creating a problem. Typically talking to the member outside of the meeting will work. The member needs to know their actions indicate they are not committed to the subject or the group. Then they can realistically work on resolving their time problem. If the member is late or leaves early due to conflicting schedules with the meeting, the member can ask the group to change meeting times or place. If the group will not change the meeting, then they need to accommodate the member by arranging the parts of the agenda that member needs to be there for during the times the member can be there.

If the member is not attending the full meeting because of lack of interest, they should suggest someone else to replace them or withdraw from being a member and accept the outcomes of the meetings without represented input. If a pager or phone calls during the meetings are the problem, members should decide if they want to agree to turn these items off during meeting times.

One way to stop late comers is to largely post the agenda before the start of the meeting and have the group agree not to change the agenda once agreement on it is complete. Because there may be important issues that come up that were not on original agenda that may need discussion, plan a fifteen to thirty minute open time near the end of the meeting for this purpose before planning the next meeting's agenda. Let group members arrive a few minutes before meeting starts and add items to this open section of the posted agenda. Then be sure to go through the agenda at start of the meeting and agree to move or reduce items on the agenda if necessary, while waiting for late comers to arrive. If there is still time left in open time, then the latecomer may add their issues onto the bottom of the list during a break or after others in open time are complete. If no open time items exist, then the meeting will end a few minutes earlier.

Another good reason for posting a visible agenda is it will reduce the need to catch members up when they miss part of the meeting. Use the visible agenda as a checklist of items completed during the meeting process. All members need to do is look at what has been checked off the agenda as complete to know where the meeting is. This prevents disruption to the meeting flow in trying to catch up a member who missed part of the meeting because they were late or had an emergency reason to leave for part of the meeting.

Growling Bears

When conflict arises between members or personal attacks start, it is important to remind the group that everyone present is valued and can provide a contribution. Bring the focus back to the subject instead of on personalities or hierarchical positions. Encourage the group to keep things constructive and moving forward, rather than on attacking one another. Try having the members take turns adding ideas or comments on the subject so the focus moves off the attackers and back to the meeting. If the arguments continue, try to help the arguing members find common ground, something they both seem to agree on but may be saying differently. If the attacks continue, ask those involved to leave their personal issues outside the meeting or if they cannot, then ask them to leave the meeting so the rest of the group may move forward. Alternatively, ask the group if they wish to continue, take a break, or dismiss the meeting since disruptive behavior may be preventing them from accomplishing their goals at this time. If the group takes a break or cancels meeting, then talk with the attackers to try to resolve whatever is keeping them from concentrating on the work that the group needs to do.

Conflict and emotion are not bad if it stays focused on the subject because it can often lead to new ideas or good compromises. However, conflict is bad for the group when it is concentrated on people or their ideas, which they may take as a personal attack or insult, instead of on the task or subject. When people feel attacked, they get defensive or withdraw from the discussion. Defensiveness will add extra time to the meeting in discussion that may not help the task and will disrupt the meeting. Withdrawal of members attacked will cheat the group out of their ideas. Withdrawal or stress due to attacks in members, even those who are not under attack, will reduce overall trust and respect for each other in meetings.

The facility environment or equipment problems can also cause discomfort to members, which may result in bad behaviors or restlessness. If environmental conditions may be the problem, find out if the room is too hot, too cold, does not have good airflow, chairs are uncomfortable, table does not fit members needs, or whatever appears to be problem in order to allow focus on meeting items. If the room temperature is the problem, give the group a short break while adjusting the room temperature. Chairs and table problems may have to be future meeting considerations unless an option for adjustments or exchanges exist. If the environmental adjustments are not possible, ask the group if another facility or date would be better to continue the tasks of the meeting.

Rabbit Trails

Sometimes in meetings, someone will say something that sparks something else that is not part of the meeting purpose. The members get going on the new subject and forget about their meeting purpose or current agenda item. When this happens the facilitator will need to remind members why they are there and ask if they need to change the focus of the meeting, add the topic as an agenda item or as an issue for later discussion, or should they return to the primary meeting purpose. Often pointing to the agenda or record of what the group has accomplished on boards or paper will return the groups focus to their original purpose. If the group agrees not to pursue the new item, then suggest putting the item in the open time for the meeting or on an issues board or parking lot to be part of a future meeting. Be sure to refer back to the issue when planning future meeting agendas.

Repeating Crow

Sometimes a member will feel that the group is not hearing their idea or input or that their point is so important that they may keep repeating it until it gets acknowledgement or agreement. To keep members from repeating their ideas, points, or arguments, utilize a board, large paper or other visible device to capture every input. This way everyone feels they have been heard and acknowledged in writing, and therefore will not feel the need to keep saying the same thing until they feel they have been heard. If members continue to repeat themselves even after the item is in writing, point out that the idea or issue is on the record. Then focus attention elsewhere by asking a related question of another individual, submitting a topic question to the group, or returning to the agenda for a review of where the group currently is in their agreed upon process.

Sleeping Possums

When there is silence in a group, a desire to fill the silence may come from the facilitator or an impatient member. However, silence can be an indication that the group is thinking about the subject at hand. If some members are close to the subject, they may be trying to view it from the perspective of someone who just brought up a new idea. Allow the group a few minutes of silent contemplation before proceeding. Typically, a member will break the silence with an idea that occurred to them during the thinking process. If no ideas or suggestions occur, then after the few minutes, ask if the group is ready to continue.

Silence can also be an indicator that the group is tired or has lost interest in the subject. If this appears to be the case, ask the group if they would like to take a break and then come back and continue. If the group wants the break, take ten to fifteen minutes and then return to the meeting agenda. If the group does not want a break, find out if they want to allow a little thinking time or free discussion on the topic before noting anything else on the record. On the other hand, they might prefer to set the topic aside for now and move onto something else on their agenda.

Sly Fox

Members, who have not had training in team building or do not understand the value of other members input, may interrupt while others are talking with their own ideas or opinions. They may also try to rephrase what someone says thinking they are being helpful or trying to manipulate statements as support for their view, when they could be wrong. These members need to be made to understand that everyone's input is important and they should wait until the person has finished their thought to ask questions or respect the agreed upon process and do it that way until group agrees to change the process. If they are trying to rephrase someone else's words for understanding or manipulation, they should verify with that person that is what they were trying to say rather than assume they know. If the member originally stating the item meant something other than what the rephrasing says, the originator should try to clarify what their meaning is. The perception of this interrupting member to the others in the group might be that they are overbearing or underhanded if their awareness of these signs of disrespect towards other members does not increase.

Timid Mouse

Members who do not participate could be not participating for a number of reasons. These reasons could include: do not feel linked to current subject, do not want to be at meeting, do not feel they have anything to contribute, person is shy, individual feels attacked or under-valued, or they prefer to think things out before jumping in. Try to bring this person into the discussion by asking a question while looking directly at them or try going around the group and having everyone contribute something. If this does not work, outside the meetings try to find out what the reason for non-participation is and come up with a way to resolve the problem. Be sure all meeting members know the importance of their input and participation at the beginning of each meeting. Everyone should learn to listen closely to others so each knows their input is both valuable and important. Be sure to thank everyone for ideas and contributions at the end of each meeting as well.

Wise Owl

Occasionally an expert will be part of a meeting and they want to share everything they know about the topic. Too much detail sometimes can bog down the group. The facilitator should watch the group's body language for when their thoughts are drifting due to too much data. When this becomes the case, then the facilitator should ask the person talking to wait and check with the group to see if they feel they know enough to proceed. If the group feels they have enough information, then the meeting should move forward. If they do not feel they have enough, then the facilitator should point to the agenda and ask how they would like to change it to move forward or if the expert could provide a memo or report to be read outside the meeting for discussion in a future meeting.

Wolf Pack

Occasionally in a meeting, some members will create their own little group within the larger group and talk to each other, which distracts from the meeting. Alternatively, they form some sort of alliance to try to get things to go their way. If the smaller group is distracting or disrupting the large group, ask everyone to focus on the subject at hand and not have separate discussions. If the disruption continues, look directly at the disrupters when asking questions to encourage their participation. If this does not work, talk to the disruptors during a break or outside the meeting. It could be they do not notice they keep talking to each other rather than the group or they may be preoccupied with another task. Making the disruptors aware of what they are doing may help them to participate better. If they continue to talk during the meeting, then the facilitator or member may have to ask them to take their discussion outside so the other members are not distracted from the focus of the meeting.

If forming the little group is an alliance to push through something in the meeting, then those alliance members need to become aware that everyone is to participate equally so all ideas can be heard and the best solution implemented. Usually the alliance is experts or old-timers on the job who feel their place or responsibility is under threat by the creation of the group or decision to discuss a particular topic. If this is the case, be sure the members of the alliance know their expertise and input is valued or they would not be part of the meetings. Point out that all the meeting members have a stake in the solution and that mutual trust and respect is important to achieving the goal.

When can you tell that the meeting process is better than it was before?

When you use the R.A!R.A! approach, your meetings will be noticeably more productive. However, if you want to verify the meeting has gone well or track the effectiveness of continuous meetings, you should consider taking some time for evaluation. The evaluation process can show your group what it is doing well and where it may still need work.

Summary

This book gave insight into meeting roles and related skills, as well as helpful tips and formats for preparation and follow-up. Applying skills learned in this book will make for meetings that are more efficient and effective. Using the R.A!R.A! approach should increase meeting accomplishments and make them more enjoyable. Meeting members should no longer feel time was wasted in meetings and increase their sense of belonging and group success.

Remember, successful meetings accomplish the desired results (tasks assigned, problems resolved, ideas generated, decisions made) while people are working together as a group using an agreed upon process. Not everyone will always be happy about the outcome of a meeting, but if the meeting process is results-oriented and decisions are typically by consensus, then most members attending the meeting will feel they contributed and the time was worthwhile.

Basic Principles

When holding meetings, remember to follow the principles of Meeting Management:.
- **All members must agree on the meeting purpose, agenda, and desired accomplishments.**
- **All members must agree on how to accomplish the purpose(s) of the meeting.**
- **All members must be willing to take action in and outside of the meeting in order to accomplish the purpose(s) of the meeting.**

Do not forget these additional principles when trying to manage meetings.
- **During meetings, everyone must have a role to play and the group must understand the purpose of each role.**
- **If the meeting has no goal to accomplish or no agenda, then the meeting has no real purpose.**
- **Meeting records are important to achieve problem resolution and track results.**

R.A!R.A! Affect

Using only the A's in the R.A!R.A! approach, which is the processes of Agenda and Actions, has been known to influence the increased productivity of some meetings by a significant amount. When adding the two R's of Roles and Records, it makes for even greater effectiveness of meeting accomplishments and group results. Using the R.A!R.A! approach will make meetings increasingly better and using all the suggestions in this book should make for excellent meetings; however, no meeting is perfect even if it scores as such on some type of evaluation. To insure meetings continue to be productive and the group becomes even more effective, in addition to learning about meetings, recommendations for the group learning is to use various problem solving methodologies and decision-making techniques. If meetings often revolve around projects, then consider reading or learning more about project management.

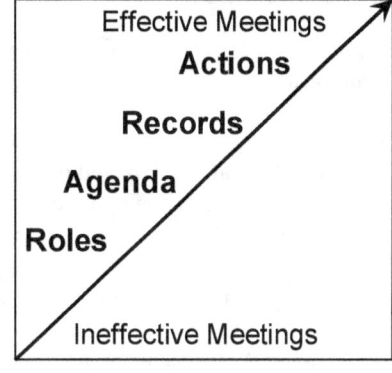

Evaluation

A meeting evaluation is a good way to tell when meeting process needs work or roles should be better defined or utilized. A good evaluation will tell the group where they need improvement and what they are doing well. The evaluation can be as simple as using a large sheet of paper or writing board at the end of a meeting to record group response to what went well and what needs improvement. Alternatively, an evaluation can be a form completed by each member and then tallied in the meeting for review or the results placed in the minutes. Use of a standard evaluation form is good if a group wants to keep a record of how they are improving or where some anonymity is desirable to insure honest feedback. To track improvement well, the measurement tool or process must remain the same throughout the tracking period. If a group finds they are not improving or doing worse when an evaluation is used, it may indicate they need additional training in meeting processes or problem solving. On the other hand, it may indicate they would work better with an impartial facilitator, who is not part of their regular group. However, the best way to tell meetings are better and people are more involved is to look at group accomplishments inside and outside of the meetings.

Example Evaluation

Below is what a single member's completed meeting evaluation might look like.

Meeting Evaluation	
Ratings: 1=Excellent, 2=Above Average, 3=Average, 4=Below Average, 5= Bad	
Statement	**Rating**
Roles	
1. Facilitator kept members focused and encouraged participation.	2
2. Members all participated in the process and took actions as appropriate.	3
3. Recorder clearly captured data and aided group progress.	1
4. Observers/Talkers knew their role and met that objective.	1
Process	
5. An agenda was prepared, reviewed, and accomplished within start/end timeframe.	1
6. Methods for idea generation, problem solving, and/or decision-making worked.	3
7. Processes to be used were agreed upon and adhered to fully.	4
8. Action items and next meeting agenda identified.	2
9. The pace of the meeting was appropriate for purpose (not too slow or too fast).	3
10. The meeting accomplished its primary purpose.	2

If the meeting had nine members using a facilitator and recorder, below is what the summary of that meeting's evaluations might look like.

Member # Question Number	#1	#2	#3	#4	#5	#6	#7	#8	#9	Average By Question
Q 1	2	2	1	1	2	3	1	1	1	1.6
Q 2	3	2	2	2	2	3	2	2	3	2.3
Q 3	1	2	1	2	1	2	1	2	1	1.4
Q 4	1	1	1	2	2	3	2	1	1	1.6
Q 5	1	1	1	2	1	3	1	1	1	1.3
Q 6	3	2	2	2	2	4	2	2	1	2.2
Q 7	4	2	3	2	2	3	2	2	1	2.3
Q 8	2	1	1	2	1	3	1	2	1	1.6
Q 9	3	3	3	2	3	4	1	3	3	2.8
Q10	2	1	2	1	2	1	1	2	1	1.4
Average by Member	2.2	1.7	1.7	1.8	1.8	2.9	1.4	1.8	1.4	**Overall** **1.9**

Briefing Evaluation Format

Ratings: 1=Excellent, 2=Above Average, 3=Average, 4=Below Average, 5=Bad	
Statement	Rating
Facilities/Equipment	
1. The room size and/or setup were appropriate.	
2. Chairs and writing surfaces were comfortable.	
3. Environmental conditions (heat, air, light, sound, etc.) were satisfactory.	
4. Necessary equipment and display options were available.	
Presentations	
5. The talker(s) was prepared and knowledgeable.	
6. The topic(s) contributed to the overall purpose.	
7. Accompanying materials and/or visuals contributed to the topic(s).	
8. Amble time was allotted for Questions and Answers	
9. The pace of the briefing was appropriate for purpose (not too slow or too fast).	

Meeting Evaluation Format

Ratings: 1=Excellent, 2=Above Average, 3=Average, 4=Below Average, 5= Bad	
Statement	Rating
Roles	
1. Facilitator kept members focused and encouraged participation.	
2. Members all participated in the process and took actions as appropriate.	
3. Recorder clearly captured data and aided group progress.	
4. Observers/Talkers knew their role and met that objective.	
Process	
5. An agenda was prepared, reviewed, and accomplished within start/end timeframe.	
6. Methods for idea generation, problem solving, and/or decision-making worked.	
7. Processes to be used were agreed upon and adhered to fully.	
8. Action items and next meeting agenda identified.	
9. The pace of the meeting was appropriate for purpose (not too slow or too fast).	
10. The meeting accomplished its primary purpose.	

If using Effectiveness Scale as noted in Introduction: 5=20% , 4=40% , 3=60% , 2= 80% , 1=100%

* NOTE: It is permissible to copy this form for meeting/ briefing use as practice. *
R.A!R.A! A Meeting Wizard's Approach

Review

1. All members must agree on the meeting _____, agenda, and desired accomplishments.
2. A basic principle of meeting management is that members must agree on how to _____ the purpose(s) of the meeting.
3. _____ are held to pull together a group of people for sharing information where participation is typically not expected.
4. The most desirable method or group decision-making is _____ .
5. The most popular method for generating a list in a meeting is _____ .
6. Types of planning meetings include _____ and Strategic.
7. A _____ is someone who leads the meeting process and insures that it flows according to the agenda and they may offer suggestions for how to proceed by suggesting methods or processes to use.
8. People who are active participants in the meeting and who understand the problem or issue are group _____ .
9. A _____ is a person who records items on large sheets of paper or writing boards and this person may be responsible for taking and publishing minutes.
10. In preparing for a meeting, be sure to schedule the meeting at the best time and _____ for the group members.
11. Using a meeting _____ for typical setups can make meeting planning easier.
12. Send _____ to people who have something to contribute to the meeting's purpose or are regular members of a group.
13. Send a meeting _____ at least two days prior to each meeting.
14. When a meeting needs to stay focused on and to accomplish it's purpose, as well as start and end on time, then to develop an _____ .
15. The three T's in an agenda refer to the Talker, the _____ , and the Time limits for each item.
16. To insure items are _____ , use writing boards or paper flip charts to record meeting progress.
17. _____ serve as a record of what happened in the meeting and who is responsible for actions items from the meeting.
18. The three W's of action items are _____ should do the task, What is the task, and When should it be done by.
19. When a problem occurs in a meeting, it usually throws the meeting off and creates high levels of _____ for some members.
20. A good _____ will tell the group where they need improvement and what they are doing well.

* NOTE: Review answers may be found on the resources page.

Final Thoughts

Meetings - Madness or Sanity?

The worst meetings I've ever seen
Accomplish absolutely nothing.
They last too many hours
And leave us feeling most sour.

The best meetings I've attended
Run quickly, smoothly,
And leave none offended.
Through careful planning,
They accomplish their task,
Even where problems
And solutions are unmasked.

My favorite meeting I'll tell
Was the one not held…
It allowed me more time
To handle goals of mine.

- Shirley Lee 01/23/03

Resources For More Information

Books

Burleson, Clyde W., *Effective Meetings: The Complete Guide.*
New York: John Wiley & Sons, Inc., 1990

DeBernardis, Frank and Frank O'Connor. *Meetings: Manage the Meeting
and You'll Manage the Company.* New York: Richardson & Steirman, Inc., 1986

Doyle, Michael and David Straus. *How to Make Meetings Work: The New Interaction
Method.* New York: Jove Books, 1982

Jeary, Tony and George Lowe. *The Secrets of Meeting Magic Revealed.*
Dallas: Walk the Talk Company, 2001

Paul, Kevin. *Chairing a Meeting with Confidence.*
Bellingham: Self-Council Press, 1989

Web Sites

Author of R.A!R.A!	www.ShirleyFineLee.com
International Association of Facilitators	www.iaf-world.org
National Association of Parliamentarians	www.parliamentarians.org
Robert's Rules of Order	www.rulesonline.com
The Facilitator Newsletter	www.thefacilitator.com
World Time Zones	www.worldtimezone.net

Review Answers
1. Purpose, 2. Accomplish, 3.Briefings, 4. Consensus, 5. Brainstorming, 6. Project,
7. Facilitator, 8. Members, 9. Recorder, 10. Place/Location, 11. Checklist, 12. Invitations,
13. Reminder, 14. Agenda, 15. Topic, 16. Captured/Recorded, 17. Minutes, 18. Who,
19. Stress, 20. Evaluation.